MW00915386

# WORLD WAR II

## STORIES FOR CURIOUS KIDS

Inspiring Tales of Bravery and
Resilience During WWII

## STUART AKOLI

Copyright © 2024 STUART AKOLI

# TABLE OF CONTENTS

# INTRODUCTION

Have you ever wondered what it felt like to be on the beaches of Normandy on D-Day? Or how the codebreakers of Bletchley Park managed to decipher the Enigma machine? What about the bravery it took to endure the Siege of Leningrad or the strategy behind the Battle of Midway that turned the tide in the Pacific Theater?

In this book, we embark on a thrilling journey through the most pivotal and dramatic moments of World War II. We'll delve into the courageous actions, strategic decisions, and incredible stories of survival and heroism that defined this monumental conflict. Each chapter brings to life the intense experiences of soldiers, civilians, and leaders who were at the heart of these historic events.

From the harrowing escape at Dunkirk to the daring pilots of the Battle of Britain, the covert operations of the Resistance, and the pivotal confrontations in the Pacific, this collection of stories captures the essence of a world at war. You'll meet the diverse characters who played crucial roles, from famous generals to unsung heroes, and discover the profound impact their actions had on the course of history.

Prepare to be captivated by the gripping tales of bravery, sacrifice, and resilience. Whether it's the relentless defense during the Blitz, the strategic genius at Stalingrad, or the groundbreaking development of the atomic bomb, each story is a testament to the indomitable human spirit in the face of adversity.

Join us as we explore these extraordinary episodes and uncover the lessons they offer for today and the future.

# STORY 1:

# What Sparked the Start of World War II?

In the late 1930s, tensions were rising in Europe. Nazi Germany, led by Adolf Hitler, had been gaining power and had already invaded and taken over several countries. On September 1, 1939, Hitler made a fateful decision that would change the world forever – he invaded Poland, marking the beginning of World War II.

The Invasion of Poland was a surprise attack by Germany that was carried out with great speed and aggression. German forces crossed the Polish border, launching air raids and ground assaults simultaneously. This invasion was a violation of international agreements and sparked an immediate response from the Allied powers, including France and the United Kingdom.

The Polish army, though outnumbered and ill-prepared for the sudden onslaught, fought bravely. However, the German military was far superior in terms of equipment and strategy. Within weeks, Poland was overrun, and the Polish government and military forces were forced to surrender. The rapid defeat of Poland shocked the world and set the stage for the devastating war that would follow.

One of the key strategies used by the Germans was the use of "blitzkrieg," which means "lightning war" in German. This involved the coordinated and rapid movement of tanks, infantry, and air support, overwhelming the enemy's defenses. This new style of warfare, combined with the superior firepower of the German army, allowed them to conquer Poland swiftly.

The Invasion of Poland had far-reaching consequences. It resulted in the formation of the Allies, a group of nations committed to fighting against the Axis powers, which were led by Germany, Italy, and Japan. The United Kingdom and France, both shocked by the ease with which Poland had been defeated, declared war on Germany in response to the invasion. This marked the official beginning of World War II.

The invasion also led to the brutal occupation of Poland by Nazi Germany. The Polish people endured widespread persecution, with the Nazis implementing harsh policies against Jews, intellectuals, and anyone they deemed a threat. The occupation lasted until 1945 and resulted in the deaths of millions of Polish civilians.

The Invasion of Poland was a pivotal moment in history. It was the event that set the world on course for one of the deadliest conflicts in human history – World War II. It revealed the ruthless tactics of Hitler's Germany and the need for the international community to unite against aggression and tyranny.

Today, we remember the brave soldiers and civilians who fought and suffered during the Invasion of Poland. Their sacrifice served as a powerful reminder of the importance of standing up for freedom, justice, and peace. The events of 1939 continue to shape our world and remind us of the importance of learning from history to create a better future.

STUART AKOLI

# STORY 2:

# How Did the Allies Escape Dunkirk?

In the spring of 1940, during World War II, a dire situation unfolded in Dunkirk, France. The German forces launched an attack on France and Belgium, forcing the Allies, including soldiers from Britain, France, and Belgium, to retreat towards the coast. With their backs against the English Channel, these soldiers found themselves trapped and in desperate need of rescue.

The soldiers were scattered along the beaches of Dunkirk, awaiting help. Their situation was grave, with enemy forces closing in and the possibility of being captured or killed looming over them. Their only hope was a daring and audacious evacuation plan.

Due to the shallow waters along the beaches, larger British naval vessels found it challenging to reach the shoreline. Thus, an urgent plea was made for small civilian boats to assist in the rescue effort. The response from fishermen, pleasure craft owners, and ordinary people was overwhelming, showing their willingness to risk their lives to save their fellow countrymen.

The evacuation, codenamed Operation Dynamo, commenced on May 26, 1940. It was a dangerous endeavor, as the troops had to remain exposed on the beaches, vulnerable to air attacks by the German Luftwaffe. However, with incredible bravery and determination, the small boats shuttled soldiers from the beaches to the larger ships waiting further out in the English Channel.

The rescue operation faced numerous challenges. The shallow waters made it difficult for the larger ships to approach and offload the soldiers they had rescued. Therefore, the British Navy utilized their destroyers to pick up soldiers directly from the beaches. Throughout the evacuation, German planes targeted the rescue vessels, subjecting them to bombing raids.

Despite these difficulties, the evacuation persisted for an entire week. The small boats tirelessly transported soldiers to safety as ordinary civilians navigated perilously close to enemy fire. Their extraordinary efforts saved countless lives and demonstrated the strength of the human spirit in the face of adversity.

By June 4, 1940, over 338,000 soldiers had been rescued from the beaches of Dunkirk. While some equipment and supplies had to be left behind, the successful evacuation marked a major strategic victory. It ensured that a significant portion of the Allied forces remained intact, ready to fight another day.

The evacuation of Dunkirk stands as a symbol of hope, resilience, and the strength of the human spirit during times of hardship. It exemplifies the power of ordinary people coming together to achieve extraordinary feats. The courage and selflessness shown by the boat owners who risked their lives to aid their fellow countrymen serve as a testament to the indomitable spirit that emerged during the darkest days of World War II.

Today, Dunkirk serves as a reminder of the sacrifices made during the war and the importance of unity and solidarity in times of crisis. The bravery of those involved in the evacuation will forever be remembered in history as a shining example of heroism and compassion.

# STORY 3:

# What Was the Blitz and How Did Britain Survive?

In 1940, during World War II, the United Kingdom came under attack by Nazi Germany. This period of intense bombing is known as the Blitz. The word "blitz" comes from the German word "Blitzkrieg," which means "lightning war."

The Blitz began on September 7, 1940, when the German Luftwaffe (the German Air Force) launched a massive air raid on London. For the next eight months, British cities were subjected to almost daily bombings. The Germans targeted not only London but also other major cities such as Coventry, Birmingham, and Liverpool.

The goal of the Blitz was to break the morale of the British people and force the British government to surrender. The German planes targeted industrial areas, factories, and infrastructure, but they also attacked residential areas, hoping to instill fear and panic among the civilians.

During the bombings, people had to take cover in shelters or underground stations to protect themselves from the onslaught. Many children were evacuated from the cities to safer areas in the countryside. People were scared, but they showed incredible resilience and bravery in the face of danger.

One of the most iconic symbols of the Blitz was the resilience of the people of London. Despite the constant bombing, life went on. The Underground, London's subway system, became a shelter for thousands of people during raids. People slept on the platforms and even used the tunnels as makeshift homes. The phrase "Keep Calm and Carry On" became a mantra for the British people, encouraging them to stay strong and continue their daily routines.

Along with the resilience of the people, another hero emerged during the Blitz: the air raid wardens. These brave men and women patrolled the streets during bombings, ensuring that people were safely inside shelters. They wore distinctive uniforms and helmets and carried whistles, which they used to signal the "all clear" after a raid.

Despite the bombs falling from the sky, the important landmarks of London, such as St. Paul's Cathedral and Buckingham Palace, remained standing. This became a symbol of hope and resilience for the British people.

The Blitz was a devastating time for the United Kingdom. In total, over 40,000 civilians were killed, and more than a million homes were destroyed or damaged. However, the German bombing campaign did not break the spirit of the British people. Instead, it strengthened their determination to fight and ultimately led to their victory in the war.

The Blitz finally came to an end in May 1941 when the Germans turned their attention towards the Soviet Union. Although the bombings had caused immense damage and loss, the British people had proven that they were unbreakable.

The Blitz remains an important part of World War II history, highlighting the courage and resilience of the British people during a time of great adversity. The stories and memories of the Blitz continue to remind us of the strength of the human spirit in the face of unimaginable challenges.

# STORY 4:

# How Did Britain Defend Against the Luftwaffe?

In 1940, during the early years of World War II, Germany had successfully conquered several countries in Europe. However, they faced one major obstacle before they could dominate the continent - Britain. Adolf Hitler, the leader of Nazi Germany, believed that if he could defeat the British, he could achieve total victory in Europe.

To invade Britain, Hitler knew he needed control of the skies. So, he ordered the German air force, known as the Luftwaffe, to launch a massive bombing campaign against the United Kingdom. This became known as the Battle of Britain.

The battle began in July 1940 and lasted until

October. The Luftwaffe aimed to destroy the Royal Air Force (RAF), the British air force, and gain air superiority over the country. They launched intense attacks on British airfields, radar stations, cities, and naval targets - all vital locations in their plan to weaken British defenses.

The RAF, under the leadership of Air Chief Marshal Sir Hugh Dowding, faced a formidable challenge. The brave pilots of the RAF, known as the "Few," fought with great determination and courage to defend their skies. They flew iconic aircraft like the Spitfire and the Hurricane, which became symbols of British resilience and bravery.

Every day, the pilots of the RAF engaged in fierce aerial battles against the German planes. They utilized their skill and training to outmaneuver and shoot down enemy aircraft. The bravery of these pilots cannot be overstated - they risked their lives to protect their country.

During the Battle of Britain, the Luftwaffe dropped thousands of bombs on Britain. Cities, towns, and villages all came under attack. London, in particular, suffered extensive bombings. The attacks caused significant damage and loss of life, but the British people displayed immense resilience.

Civilians in Britain showed courage and perseverance as they faced the constant threat of destruction from above. They sought refuge in shelters, such as the underground subway stations known as the Tube, where they would take shelter during air raids. Their spirit of "Keep Calm and Carry On" became a symbol of British resolve during the war.

As the battle continued, the RAF resisted the Luftwaffe's attacks with great bravery. The British pilots, with their superior training and aircraft, ultimately gained an advantage. They proved to be a formidable opponent, shooting down enough enemy planes to force Hitler to abandon his plans to invade Britain.

The Battle of Britain was a critical turning point in the war. British victory not only thwarted Germany's plans for invasion but also boosted the morale of the Allied forces and provided hope for the future. Winston Churchill, the British Prime Minister, famously said, "Never in the field of human conflict was so much owed by so many to so few."

The Battle of Britain stands as a testament to the courage and determination of the British people and the RAF pilots. Their heroic defense of their country against overwhelming odds is remembered as one of the greatest stories of World War II.

# STORY 5:

# Who Were the Brave Fighters in the Resistance?

During World War II, many countries in Europe were occupied by the Nazis. However, the people of these countries did not simply accept Nazi rule. They formed secret underground movements called Resistance Movements to fight against the Nazis and help their countries regain their freedom.

The Resistance Movements were comprised of courageous men and women from all walks of life, including students, farmers, teachers, doctors, and factory workers. Their main objective was to gather information about the Nazis and their plans, as well as to sabotage their operations whenever possible.

One notable group of resistance fighters was the

French Resistance. They operated covertly to sabotage Nazi efforts, such as destroying bridges and railways, disrupting communication lines, and gathering intelligence. Among their most famous acts of defiance was the detonation of a significant Nazi ammunition depot in Paris, severely impeding German military capabilities.

In Norway, a group called the Norwegian Resistance emerged. They aided Allied pilots who had been shot down, providing them with shelter and counterfeit passports to facilitate their return to their own countries. They also gathered information about German military movements and shared it with the Allies.

In Poland, the Polish Resistance fiercely fought against the Nazis. One of their most courageous acts was the Warsaw Ghetto Uprising. The Nazis had forced Jews into tightly controlled areas known as ghettos, subjecting the inhabitants to horrendous conditions. In 1943, when the Nazis attempted to deport the remaining Jews in the Warsaw Ghetto to concentration camps, the resistance fighters fought back for nearly a month, surprising the Nazis with their determination and bravery.

The Resistance Movements faced great risks. If members were captured by the Nazis, they would be subject to severe torture and could even face execution. Nevertheless, many brave individuals were willing to sacrifice their lives to protect their countries and defeat the Nazis.

Some resistance fighters were able to provide crucial information to the Allies. One well-known group called the Dutch Underground, had a spy named Christiaan Lindemans, who gathered invaluable intelligence about German rocket technology. His information aided the Allies in planning a successful bombing raid, preventing further Nazi rocket attacks.

The Resistance Movements were not exclusive to Western Europe. In the Soviet Union, partisans fought against German occupation forces. They disrupted German supply lines, gathered intelligence, and carried out guerrilla attacks. The Soviet partisans played a vital role in weakening German forces on the Eastern Front.

The work of the Resistance Movements was dangerous and often went unknown by the Nazis. Nevertheless, their efforts were not in vain. They not only saved countless lives but also provided valuable support to the Allied forces, helping pave the way for the ultimate defeat of the Nazis.

The bravery and determination of the resistance fighters serve as a reminder that even in the darkest of times, there are always individuals willing to stand up for what is right. Their stories inspire us and teach us the importance of never giving up and fighting for freedom and justice.

The Resistance Movements played a crucial role in the defeat of the Nazis and the liberation of Europe. Their courage and unwavering commitment to their cause will forever be remembered as a shining example of the human spirit in the face of adversity.

# STORY 6:

# Why Did Germany Invade the Soviet Union?

In the summer of 1941, a colossal invasion known as Operation Barbarossa commenced. This significant military campaign was carried out by Germany against the Soviet Union during World War II. More than just a battle, Operation Barbarossa was a massive undertaking that witnessed the clash of two powerful nations.

On June 22, 1941, without any prior warning, German forces launched a surprise attack on the Soviet Union. The attack's objective was to conquer large portions of Soviet territory and eliminate the Soviet government. Hitler's plan involved swiftly capturing Moscow and Leningrad (now Saint Petersburg), as well as seizing control of Ukraine's agricultural resources.

The Soviet Union was taken off guard by the sudden onslaught. Despite having some intelligence about a potential German attack, Soviet leader Joseph Stalin and his advisors failed to anticipate the scale and ferocity of the German offensive fully. The initial assault left Soviet troops disorganized and bewildered, struggling to defend their homeland.

The German forces surged forward, rapidly capturing vast territories and seizing key cities such as Minsk and Kyiv. Their swift advances alarmed the Soviets, who desperately tried to regroup and form defensive lines. The German army employed powerful tanks, aircraft, and well-coordinated tactics, making them a formidable adversary.

Although initially caught off guard, the Soviet people and their military did not surrender easily. The Red Army launched counterattacks to slow down the German advance, inflicting heavy casualties upon the invaders. Furthermore, the harsh Russian winter conditions also played a significant role in slowing down the German offensive, as they were unprepared for the extreme cold.

As the Germans pushed further into Soviet territory, the local population formed partisan resistance movements. These courageous civilians fought back against the invaders, sabotaging supply lines, gathering intelligence, and launching surprise attacks. This partisan warfare greatly hindered the German occupation, forcing them to divert resources toward combating the resistance.

The tide of the battle started to turn at the Battle of Stalingrad from late 1942 to early 1943. This brutal battle witnessed some of the most intense fighting, with both sides suffering tremendous losses. The Soviet Union successfully defended the city, inflicting a significant defeat on the German forces. Stalingrad became a symbol of Soviet resilience and marked a turning point in the war.

Following the Battle of Stalingrad, the Soviet Union launched a series of offensives, unleashing a relentless counterattack against the German invaders. The Red Army gradually regained lost territory, pushing the Germans back towards Germany. The Soviet Union's resilience and determination proved to be crucial in halting the German advance.

Operation Barbarossa was a significant turning point in World War II. While initially successful, the German invasion of the Soviet Union ultimately failed due to the Soviets' tenacity and determination. The Soviet Union's vast resources, harsh climate, and refusal to surrender proved instrumental in repelling the German forces. The invasion taught a valuable lesson: even the most meticulously planned military campaigns can be met with fierce resistance.

# STORY 7:

# What Happened at Pearl Harbor?

On the morning of December 7, 1941, a beautiful Sunday in Hawaii, the peaceful atmosphere was suddenly shattered by the sound of explosions and the sight of Japanese planes soaring through the sky. This was the day that the United States was pulled into World War II.

Pearl Harbor, located on the island of Oahu, was a vital U.S. naval base in the Pacific. At around 7:55 a.m., over 350 Japanese fighter planes, bombers, and torpedo planes launched a surprise attack on the harbor. The Japanese aimed to cripple the American Pacific Fleet in a single blow, allowing Japan to expand its territory unchecked.

The attack began with a wave of bombs raining down on the ships docked at Pearl Harbor. The USS Arizona, a battleship, was hit by several bombs, causing a massive explosion. Trapped sailors desperately tried to escape the sinking ship, but tragically, over a thousand crew members lost their lives on the Arizona alone.

Other ships, including the USS Oklahoma and USS West Virginia, were also severely damaged or sunk during the attack. The USS Nevada managed to escape the harbor but was heavily damaged. The USS California, USS Maryland, USS Tennessee, and USS Pennsylvania were hit but managed to survive.

As the Japanese planes returned for a second wave of attacks, they focused on the military airfields at Hickam, Wheeler, and Bellows. They intentionally targeted the hangars, aircraft, and fuel supplies to ensure that the U.S. military's ability to respond would be hampered.

The devastation was not limited to the naval base. The attack also targeted army bases, including Schofield Barracks and Fort Shafter, resulting in significant casualties and damage. The surprise nature of the attack left military personnel and civilians little time to react or escape the destruction.

Within two hours, the Japanese had achieved their objective. The once-mighty American Pacific Fleet lay in ruins, with over 2,400 Americans killed and more than 1,200 injured. The attack on Pearl Harbor was a tremendous blow to the United States, but it also rallied the country to unite and fight back against Japan.

The next day, President Franklin D. Roosevelt addressed Congress, declaring December 7, 1941, "a date which will live in infamy" and urging Congress to declare war on Japan. The United States officially entered World War II, joining forces with the Allied Powers against the Axis Powers, which included Germany and Italy.

The attack on Pearl Harbor shocked and angered Americans across the nation. It galvanized their determination to support the war effort. Men enlisted in the military, women joined the workforce, and citizens on the home front worked together to contribute to the war in various ways.

It was not until August 15, 1945, that Japan would finally surrender, marking the end of the war in the Pacific. The Pearl Harbor attack served as a turning point in American history, propelling a nation into war and shaping the course of the war itself.

Decades after the attack, the remains of the USS Arizona still lie beneath the waters of Pearl Harbor, serving as a memorial to the lives lost that fateful day. Today, the USS Arizona Memorial stands above the ship, reminding visitors of the importance of remembering the sacrifices made during World War II.

# STORY 8:

# How Did Leningrad Endure the Siege?

During World War II, a tragic and devastating event unfolded in the city known at the time as Leningrad, which is now called Saint Petersburg, Russia. This event, known as the Siege of Leningrad, lasted for approximately 900 days, from September 8, 1941, to January 27, 1944.

When Nazi Germany launched its invasion of the Soviet Union in 1941, one of its key objectives was to capture Leningrad. The city held significant strategic importance as a major industrial and cultural center. The Nazis believed that capturing Leningrad would severely weaken the Soviet Union.

To achieve their goal, the German army, in collaboration with their Finnish allies, encircled

Leningrad and cut off all supply routes, imposing a deadly blockade. The people living in Leningrad found themselves trapped and isolated from the outside world. The Nazis intentionally sought to starve the city into surrender.

Life within Leningrad during the siege became incredibly challenging. The scarcity of food, fuel, and other essential supplies quickly became dire. The population endured long, freezing lines for meager rations, often consisting of small pieces of bread. Desperation led many to consume whatever they could find, including rats and pets, while some even resorted to boiling leather shoes. These harsh conditions resulted in widespread hunger and disease.

Despite these extreme hardships, the people of Leningrad displayed incredible resilience and courage. Community kitchens were organized, where resources were pooled to cook meals and share food. Medical professionals tirelessly cared for the sick and injured, working with limited supplies. Artists, musicians, and writers continued to create, using their talents to uplift the spirits of the people.

The Soviet government played a crucial role in supporting the resistance effort. Soviet leader Joseph

Stalin declared Leningrad a "hero city" and dispatched additional troops and supplies to bolster the city's defense. The defenders of Leningrad pushed back against the German forces, often paying a great price in lives lost.

Throughout the siege, the city was subjected to relentless bombing and shelling by the German army. The residents of Leningrad lived in constant fear as danger lurked around every corner. Nevertheless, they persevered. Makeshift shelters were constructed, and people dug trenches to protect themselves from the bombs.

The harsh winter of 1941-1942 brought additional challenges. The Nazis had hoped that the bitter cold and scarcity of supplies would force the city to surrender. However, the people of Leningrad braved the freezing temperatures and remained resolute in their resistance.

In 1943, the tide of the war began to shift in favor of the Soviet Union. The Red Army launched a series of offensives, pushing back the German forces. Slowly, the blockade on Leningrad started to weaken.

Finally, on January 27, 1944, the siege was lifted. The German army was forced to retreat, and the people of Leningrad celebrated their hard-fought victory. Nevertheless, the cost was tremendously high. It is estimated that around 1 million civilians and soldiers lost their lives during the siege, making it one of the deadliest battles in history.

The Siege of Leningrad serves as a testament to the strength and determination of the human spirit. The people of Leningrad refused to succumb to the horrors of war and clung to hope during the darkest of times. Their bravery and resilience will forever be remembered as an incredible example of human endurance.

# STORY 9:

# Who Were the Tuskegee Airmen?

During World War II, a group of incredible individuals known as the Tuskegee Airmen played a significant role in the fight for freedom and justice. These remarkable men were the first African American military aviators in the U.S. Army Air Corps.

In the 1940s, racial discrimination and segregation were deeply entrenched in the United States. African Americans faced numerous challenges and were often denied equal opportunities. However, a group of determined African American military leaders believed in the potential of African Americans in aviation.

In 1941, the Tuskegee Institute in Alabama was selected to lead an experimental program to train African Americans as military pilots. The primary objective was to demonstrate that these pilots could serve their country as effectively as anyone else.

Under the leadership of Captain Benjamin O. Davis Jr., the Tuskegee Airmen embarked on a demanding training program. They encountered various obstacles, including racial prejudice from some white officers and instructors. Despite facing these challenges, the Tuskegee Airmen pressed on, displaying unwavering determination and skill.

The training encompassed both ground and flight exercises. The aspiring aviators had to master navigation, aeronautics, and the intricacies of operating complex aircraft. Additionally, they had to demonstrate physical fitness to withstand the demands of flying at high altitudes and under extreme conditions.

In 1943, the Tuskegee Airmen officially became the 99th Pursuit Squadron of the U.S. Army Air Corps. This was a monumental milestone, as it marked the first time African Americans were allowed to serve as military pilots. They swiftly proved their worth and showcased exceptional abilities in the field of aviation.

The Tuskegee Airmen were deployed to the European Theater of Operations during World War II. They undertook numerous critical missions, providing vital support to Allied forces. Despite initial concerns about their combat readiness, they demonstrated their capabilities as skilled pilots, effectively protecting bomber aircraft during dangerous missions.

The Tuskegee Airmen gained a formidable reputation for their outstanding performance in air combat. They earned the nickname "Red Tails" due to the distinctive red markings on their planes. The Red Tails were known for their camaraderie, incredible bravery, and effectiveness in air battles.

Their success shattered the prevalent myth that African Americans were incapable of becoming skilled aviators. The Tuskegee Airmen became a significant source of inspiration for many African Americans, proving that with determination and hard work, they could achieve greatness in any field.

Following the conclusion of the war, the Tuskegee

Airmen continued to break barriers between military and civilian life. Their achievements played a crucial role in the desegregation of the armed forces and contributed to the advancements of the Civil Rights Movement.

In recognition of their bravery and contributions, the Tuskegee Airmen received numerous awards and honors. In 2007, they were collectively awarded the Congressional Gold Medal, the highest civilian honor conferred by the U.S. Congress.

The legacy of the Tuskegee Airmen serves as a reminder that courage knows no boundaries. They overcame adversity and significantly impacted history. The story of the Tuskegee Airmen teaches us the importance of perseverance and the power of fighting for equality and justice. They serve as an enduring inspiration to all.

# STORY 10:

# Why Were Japanese Americans Interned?

During World War II, a significant and regrettable chapter in American history unfolded as thousands of Japanese Americans were forcibly removed from their homes and relocated to internment camps. This tragic event was fueled by fear and prejudice, which were exacerbated by the surprise attack on Pearl Harbor by Japan on December 7, 1941.

Following the attack, concerns arose among some Americans that Japanese Americans living in the United States might be acting as spies or saboteurs for Japan. Responding to these fears, the U.S. government made a controversial decision to issue an executive order known as Executive Order 9066, which ultimately led to the forced removal and internment of Japanese Americans residing primarily on the West Coast. This order authorized the relocation of Japanese Americans to internment camps in inland areas.

Approximately 120,000 Japanese Americans, two-thirds of whom were U.S. citizens, were affected by this order. They were given short notice to gather their belongings and were compelled to leave their homes, jobs, and possessions behind. Families were separated, and their lives were abruptly upended.

Life in the internment camps presented numerous challenges. The camps were often crowded, with families residing in cramped barracks and lacking privacy. Living conditions were frequently inadequate, with limited access to basic necessities such as food, healthcare, and sanitation facilities. Yet, despite these hardships, Japanese Americans strove to make the best of their circumstances and foster a sense of community within the camps.

Children also faced numerous difficulties. They had to adjust to new schools within the camps and cope with limited educational resources. Despite these challenges, many Japanese American children persisted in their studies and even achieved academic success in the camps.

Despite the unjust treatment they endured, some Japanese Americans still found ways to serve their country. Numerous young men volunteered to join the U.S. Army, forming the 442nd Regimental Combat Team. This all-Japanese American unit became one of the most decorated units in U.S. military history, displaying their loyalty and bravery in battle.

It wasn't until 1944 that the U.S. government began to acknowledge the unfairness of the internment policy. In the case of Korematsu v. United States, the Supreme Court made a significant decision, ruling that the internment of Japanese Americans was constitutional due to military necessity. However, this decision was later widely criticized as unjust, and in 1988, the U.S. government officially apologized and provided reparations to surviving Japanese American internees.

The internment of Japanese Americans continues to remain a painful and crucial chapter in American history. It serves as a lasting reminder of the consequences that arise from fear, prejudice, and the erosion of civil liberties during times of conflict. The experiences endured by Japanese Americans during World War II have fueled ongoing efforts to promote justice and equality for all individuals, regardless of their ethnicity or background.

Today, the internment camps have been dismantled, and the sites serve as solemn reminders of this dark period in history. They stand as a poignant reminder of the importance of safeguarding civil liberties, even in times of fear and uncertainty. History should serve as a lesson, and it is our responsibility to ensure that such injustices are never repeated.

As we continue to explore World War II, we will delve further into stories of bravery, perseverance, and the ongoing struggle against oppression. Stay curious, young readers, as we embark on more fascinating tales from history.

# STORY 11:

# How Did Code Breakers Help Win the War?

During World War II, the Germans used a complex encoding machine called the Enigma to send secret messages to their military units. These messages were difficult to decipher, as they were scrambled using a series of rotating wheels and electrical circuits. However, the Allies were determined to crack this seemingly unbreakable code. This is the incredible story of the Enigma code breakers.

In 1939, as war loomed over Europe, the Allies knew that breaking the Enigma code was crucial to gaining an advantage over the Germans. Alan Turing, a brilliant mathematician and code-breaker from Britain, was recruited to work on this top-secret project. They faced a formidable challenge, as the

Enigma machine produced numerous potential codes.

To crack the Enigma code, Turing and his team worked on developing innovative ideas and advancements, but they did not build a machine called the Turing machine. The title refers to Turing himself. Turing's groundbreaking work included developing the concept of the Universal Turing Machine, which laid the foundation for modern computers and artificial intelligence. His theoretical contributions were instrumental in the code-breaking efforts.

The code-breaking efforts were centered at Bletchley Park in England. It was here that the brightest minds from different fields came together to work on the Enigma code problem. Linguists, chess champions, mathematicians, and computer scientists all played crucial roles in deciphering the code.

To speed up the decryption process, Turing and his team worked on another machine called the Bombe. This device could process multiple possible code combinations simultaneously. It significantly reduced the time required to decrypt the German messages.

The code-breakers needed any information they could find to help decrypt the Enigma codes. They intercepted and carefully studied German military communications, looking for patterns. They analyzed weather reports, radio signals, and known phrases to piece together fragments of the code.

After months of relentless work, the code-breakers achieved a major breakthrough. They successfully decrypted German messages, providing valuable intelligence about German naval plans. This success gave them hope and motivated them to continue their efforts.

One of the most critical contributions of the Enigma code breakers was their role in the Battle of the Atlantic. By deciphering German naval codes, the Allies were able to locate and disrupt German U-boat operations, turning the tide in the battle for control of the Atlantic Ocean.

As the code-breakers became more proficient, they developed an actual machine called Colossus, not Mega. Colossus was a faster and more efficient machine that further improved the decryption process. With Colossus, the Allies could decrypt coded German messages in a matter of hours.

Secrecy was paramount throughout this operation. The code-breakers understood the importance of keeping their work hidden from the enemy. The intelligence gained through decrypting the Enigma codes proved to be incredibly valuable in planning military operations without the Germans suspecting their codes had been cracked.

The efforts of the Enigma code breakers revolutionized cryptanalysis and changed the course of the war. Turing's work on the code-breaking project laid the foundation for modern computers and artificial intelligence. Their dedication and intelligence were instrumental in shortening the war and saving countless lives.

The Enigma code breakers' accomplishments were tremendous, unlocking the secrets of German messages that had seemed indecipherable. Their efforts played a crucial role in the Allied victory during World War II. The story of these remarkable individuals is a testament to human ingenuity and the power of teamwork.

# STORY 12:

# What Happened at the Battle of Coral Sea?

In the early months of 1942, the United States and its allies were engaged in a fierce struggle with the Japanese Empire in the Pacific. The Battle of Coral Sea, fought from May 4th to May 8th, would become a significant turning point in this monumental conflict.

At the time, Japan sought to expand its empire and establish dominance in the Pacific region. Their plan included capturing Port Moresby, a strategically important location in New Guinea that would provide them with a base from which they could launch further attacks. The United States and its allies were determined to prevent this from happening.

The battle took place in the Coral Sea, located near the northeastern coast of Australia. It was a historic battle as it marked the first time in history that two fleets engaged in combat without ever seeing each other directly. Both the American and Japanese fleets relied on their carrier-based aircraft to attack their enemy.

The American forces were commanded by Admiral Frank Jack Fletcher, while the Japanese were led by Vice Admiral Takeo Takagi and Vice Admiral Shigeyoshi Inoue. The Allies had two aircraft carriers, the USS Lexington and the USS Yorktown, while the Japanese had the carriers Shokaku and Zuikaku.

On May 7th, the two sides clashed in intense air battles. American and Japanese planes launched wave after wave of attacks, each trying to gain the upper hand. The skies above the Coral Sea were filled with the roar of engines and the sound of gunfire as planes engaged in dogfights and ships fired anti-aircraft guns.

During the battle, the USS Lexington was hit by multiple bombs and torpedoes and was eventually forced to be abandoned. The USS Yorktown, though heavily damaged, managed to stay afloat thanks to the heroic efforts of its crew and the support of repair ships.

The Battle of Coral Sea was a crucial engagement that had significant impacts. While both sides suffered losses, the battle marked the first time that the Japanese advance had been halted. The Allies successfully defended Port Moresby and prevented the Japanese from achieving their objectives.

Moreover, the Battle of Coral Sea set the stage for future victories in the Pacific. It demonstrated to the Allies that the Japanese Navy could be defeated. It also established tactics and strategies that would be utilized in subsequent battles, such as the Battle of Midway.

The Battle of Coral Sea served as a turning point in the tides of war, favoring the United States and its allies. It provided a much-needed boost in morale and set the stage for the eventual defeat of Japan.

In conclusion, the Battle of Coral Sea was a critical victory in the ongoing struggle for control of the Pacific. It displayed the United States and its allies as a formidable force, paving the way for future successes. We should always remember and honor the sacrifices of the brave men and women who fought in this pivotal battle.

# STORY 13:

# How Did the Battle of Midway Turn the Tide?

The Battle of Midway was indeed a vital turning point in World War II, a naval battle fought between the United States and Japan in the central Pacific Ocean. It took place from June 4-7, 1942. Midway Island, located in the Pacific, held great strategic importance for both sides.

By June 1942, Japan had already gained control of numerous Pacific islands and had its sights set on Midway. Capturing the island would have allowed them to launch further attacks on the United States.

However, American code-breakers intercepted and decoded secret Japanese messages, revealing their plans. Admiral Chester Nimitz, the commander of the U.S. Pacific Fleet, recognized this as a golden opportunity. He devised a plan to surprise the Japanese fleet and overwhelm them.

On June 4, 1942, the American and Japanese aircraft carriers engaged in battle. The Japanese fleet consisted of four carriers, compared to the Americans' three, giving them a numerical advantage. However, the United States had an advantage through their code-breaking skills and superior intelligence.

Taking off from the aircraft carriers, U.S. planes managed to locate and attack the Japanese carriers before the Japanese were aware of their presence. In just a span of five minutes, American planes were able to sink three out of the four Japanese aircraft carriers. This was a significant blow to the Japanese, as their carriers were their most powerful weapons.

Furthermore, American dive bombers targeted other Japanese vessels, like cruisers and destroyers, causing extensive damage to the Japanese fleet. The American planes demonstrated speed, accuracy, and relentlessness.

Meanwhile, the Japanese planes faced difficulties. They received false information, and their attacks became disorganized. While the American planes wreaked havoc on the Japanese ships, the Japanese were unable to inflict significant damage on the American carriers.

The Battle of Midway lasted for three days, and by the end, the Japanese fleet was left devastated. They lost four carriers, a heavy cruiser, and over 300 aircraft. On the American side, one carrier, the USS Yorktown, was lost, along with some aircraft. However, the victory gave the U.S. Navy a much-needed boost in morale and marked a turning point in the Pacific Theater.

It is essential to note that the Battle of Midway was not just about numbers and equipment but also about intelligence and strategy. The American code-breakers played a crucial role in deciphering Japanese messages, enabling the United States to anticipate and counter the enemy's moves. This battle exemplified the significance of intelligence gathering and its potential to alter the course of the war.

The Battle of Midway remains one of the most significant naval battles in history. It showcased the strength and determination of the U.S. Navy and marked a shift in momentum in the Pacific Theater. The victory at Midway instilled newfound confidence in the United States and dispelled the notion of Japanese invincibility. From that point forward, it became evident that the tide of the war had turned in favor of the Allies.

# STORY 14:

# What Was the Manhattan Project?

During World War II, a secret project known as the Manhattan Project was underway in the United States. It was a top-secret mission with one goal in mind: to develop the atomic bomb. This weapon had the potential to change the course of the war. Here is the fascinating story of the Manhattan Project.

In the early 1940s, scientists from various countries came together in the United States to work on a top-secret mission. They were led by physicist J. Robert Oppenheimer. Their task was to harness the immense power of the atom and build a weapon that would end the war.

The team faced many challenges along the way. The first step was to find a suitable location for the project. They needed a place that was remote and away from prying eyes. Eventually, they settled in Los Alamos, a secluded area in New Mexico.

Once the location was secured, the scientists faced another hurdle: obtaining the necessary materials to build the bomb. They needed uranium and plutonium, two highly radioactive elements. The process of obtaining these materials was complex and dangerous.

To obtain uranium, the scientists relied on a process called uranium enrichment. This involved separating the uranium isotopes to increase the concentration of the fissionable isotope, which is necessary for a nuclear explosion. Plutonium, on the other hand, had to be manufactured in a nuclear reactor.

With the materials in hand, the scientists began constructing the bomb. They designed two types of atomic bombs: "Little Boy" and "Fat Man". "Little Boy" used uranium-235 and was dropped on Hiroshima, Japan, on August 6, 1945. "Fat Man" used plutonium-239 and was dropped on Nagasaki, Japan, on August 9, 1945.

The decision to use the atomic bomb was not taken lightly. The devastating power of these weapons was unlike anything the world had ever seen. However, the Allies believed that using the bomb would save lives by forcing Japan to surrender, thus bringing an end to the war.

When the bombs were dropped, the impact was immense. The cities of Hiroshima and Nagasaki were leveled, and thousands of people lost their lives. The destruction was so great that Japan surrendered just days after the bombing of Nagasaki, marking the end of World War II.

The Manhattan Project was a remarkable achievement in the scientific and engineering fields. It pushed the boundaries of what was thought possible, but it also raised serious moral questions about the use of such devastating weapons. The project had a lasting impact on the world, leading to the arms race between the United States and the Soviet Union during the Cold War.

After the war, the United States took steps to ensure that the knowledge and technology behind the atomic bomb would not fall into the wrong hands. The Atomic Energy Act of 1946 established the

United States Atomic Energy Commission to regulate the peaceful use of nuclear energy and weapons development.

In conclusion, the Manhattan Project was a secret project that played a crucial role in the development of the atomic bomb. It brought together the brightest minds in scientific research and engineering, culminating in the creation of a weapon that would change the world forever. Despite the immense destruction caused by the bombings, the project's legacy continues to shape our understanding of science, ethics, and the importance of international diplomacy.

# STORY 15:

# Why Was El Alamein a Turning Point?

The Battle of El Alamein was a crucial battle that occurred from October 23 to November 4, 1942, in North Africa during World War II. It marked a significant turning point in the war and ended the Axis threat to the Suez Canal, a vital route for transporting goods and supplies.

During this time, the Allied forces, under the command of British General Bernard Montgomery, faced off against the Axis forces, primarily composed of German and Italian troops led by General Erwin Rommel, known as the Desert Fox.

The battle unfolded near the Egyptian town of El Alamein, strategically positioned along the coast of the Mediterranean Sea. The British Eighth Army, comprised of soldiers from the United Kingdom, Australia, New Zealand, and South Africa, faced the formidable task of halting the advancing Axis forces and safeguarding the Suez Canal.

In the months preceding the battle, Rommel's troops had made significant gains in North Africa, gradually pushing back the British forces. The Axis forces were confident, believing they could continue their advance. However, Montgomery and his troops were determined to shift the balance of power in their favor.

The Battle of El Alamein commenced on October 23, 1942. Under the cover of darkness, the British forces launched a massive artillery bombardment on the Axis positions. This initial assault was followed by a coordinated ground offensive supported by tanks and aircraft.

The battle unfolded over nearly two weeks, with both sides fiercely fighting for control of the region. The British forces employed innovative tactics and strategies, including extensive minefields to impede enemy progress. The Axis forces, skilled in desert warfare, mounted a tough resistance.

As the battle progressed, the British forces gradually gained the upper hand. They successfully pushed back the Axis forces, albeit slowly. The Allied air superiority played a crucial role, with British and American aircraft bombarding Axis positions and disrupting their supply lines.

By November 4, the Axis forces were in full retreat. Realizing that his troops were outmatched, Rommel ordered a complete withdrawal. The Battle of El Alamein proved to be a decisive victory for the Allies since it not only halted the Axis advance but also significantly boosted their morale, marking a turning point in the war.

The impact of the Battle of El Alamein was profound. It effectively eliminated the Axis threat to the Suez Canal and ensured that this crucial supply line remained under Allied control. Additionally, the battle provided the Allies with a much-needed morale boost, substantiating that the Axis powers were not invincible.

The Battle of El Alamein stands as a pivotal moment in World War II, showcasing the determination and resilience of the Allied forces. It serves as a testament to the importance of strategic planning, teamwork, and innovative approaches to warfare. The battle serves as a reminder that even in the face of adversity, resilience and determination can pave the path to victory.

# STORY 16:

# Who Were the Code Talkers?

During World War II, a group of Native American soldiers played a crucial role in the war effort by using their languages to create unbreakable codes. These men, known as the Code Talkers, made significant contributions in keeping Allied communications secret from the enemy.

The idea of using Native American languages as codes originated when a military officer named Philip Johnston recognized that the complex languages spoken by tribes like the Navajo, Comanche, and Choctaw were unfamiliar to outsiders. This made them a perfect basis for creating a code that would be nearly impossible for the enemy to decipher.

Among the Native American languages, Navajo

proved to be particularly effective as a secret code language. It was unwritten and had a complex grammar structure, which made it challenging for anyone without proper training to understand. While Code Talkers were recruited from various Native American tribes, the Navajo quickly became the primary group engaged in this top-secret work.

To uphold the secrecy of their mission, the Code Talkers underwent intense training. They were instructed in military tactics, memorized a list of military terms in their native language, and learned to verbally communicate these codes quickly and accurately. The skilled Code Talkers became experts in conveying important messages in the heat of battle.

Once adequately trained, the Code Talkers were sent to different units, where they played a vital role in transmitting battlefield information. Using their native languages, they communicated messages such as troop movements, tactical strategies, and other critical information that had to be kept secret from the enemy.

The codes developed by the Code Talkers were highly effective in preventing the enemy from intercepting and comprehending Allied communications. The Axis powers, particularly the Japanese, made numerous attempts to decode these messages but were unsuccessful due to the intricate nature of the Native American languages used.

The Code Talkers served in various campaigns and battles across the Pacific Theater, including the Pacific islands and the jungles of Guadalcanal and Iwo Jima. They often fought on the frontlines, facing danger alongside their fellow soldiers.

Their contributions were invaluable to the war effort and greatly assisted in the Allied victory. The presence of the Code Talkers had a significant impact on the outcome of many battles, as secure communication allowed for better coordination between military units and strategic decision-making.

Despite their essential role in the war, the Code Talkers' efforts remained classified and top-secret until many years after the war had ended. Only in the 1960s did their contribution to the war effort become widely known. The Code Talkers were finally recognized for their valuable service and received honors and awards for their bravery and ingenuity.

The legacy of the Code Talkers is one of courage,

perseverance, and patriotism. Their linguistic skills and dedication saved countless lives and played a crucial role in securing victory for the Allies. The story of the Code Talkers serves as a powerful reminder of the diverse contributions made by Native American soldiers and their lasting impact on World War II.

# STORY 17:

# What Did Anne Frank's Diary Reveal?

During the period of 1942-1944, Anne Frank, a young Jewish girl, and her family sought refuge from the Nazis and went into hiding. They concealed themselves in a hidden annex located behind her father's office building in Amsterdam.

Joining the Franks in hiding were another family named the Van Pels, as well as a dentist named Mr. Albert Dussel. They endured cramped living conditions within the concealed space, constantly keeping their voices low during the day to avoid detection by the office workers below.

Life in hiding posed various challenges for Anne and her family. They had to ensure that the windows remained covered at all times and that movement within the annex was limited to specific periods when they knew it would not arouse suspicion. Additionally, food had to be carefully managed due to the rationing that was enforced during the war.

To occupy herself, Anne began writing in her diary. She poured her thoughts, dreams, and fears onto the pages of her diary, which she named "Kitty."

Anne's diary serves as a testament to the struggles faced by those in hiding. Any unfamiliar noises or unexpected visitors had to be approached with the utmost caution, as discovery by the Nazis would mean deportation to the concentration camps.

Despite the adversities they encountered, glimpses of hope and moments of joy emerged through Anne's words. She expressed her love for her family and shared her aspirations for the future, nurturing dreams of becoming a writer and journalist.

Furthermore, Anne's diary highlights the significance of the helpers who risked their lives to aid those in hiding. Miep Gies, one of the office assistants, played a vital role in supporting the occupants of the annex by providing food, books, and news from the outside world. Her actions provided a lifeline of hope and kept the connection with the outside intact.

Tragically, after two years of hiding, the secret annex was discovered by the Nazis. Consequently, the Franks, the Van Pels, and Mr. Dussel were arrested and sent to concentration camps. Both Anne and her sister Margot were transferred to the Bergen-Belsen camp, where they died of disease shortly before the camp's liberation.

Although Anne did not survive, her diary did. Miep Gies found the diary and delivered it to Anne's father, Otto Frank, the sole survivor of the Frank family. Otto published Anne's diary, creating an extraordinary testament to the Holocaust's horrors and offering a unique perspective into the life of a young girl caught in the midst of war.

Today, Anne's diary stands as one of the world's most widely read books, translated into over 70 languages. It continues to inspire readers of all ages with Anne's spirit, courage, and determination to hold onto hope even in the darkest of times.

Anne Frank's diary serves as an enduring reminder of the millions of innocent lives lost during the

Holocaust and the significance of standing against discrimination and hatred. Her words resonate with readers, forever reminding us of the strength of hope and the indomitable nature of the human spirit.

# STORY 18:

# What Was the Bataan Death March?

During World War II, one of the most tragic and brutal events occurred in the Philippines, known as the Bataan Death March. It was a time of great suffering and endurance for American and Filipino prisoners of war.

In the early months of 1942, the Japanese Imperial Army advanced into the Philippines. American and Filipino forces fought bravely, but they were eventually overwhelmed. On April 9, 1942, the Allied forces finally surrendered on the Bataan Peninsula.

Over 70,000 Filipino and American soldiers were taken captive by the Japanese. Their captors showed them no mercy. The prisoners were forced to march approximately 65 miles from Bataan to a Japanese prison camp at Camp O'Donnell. They were given hardly any food or water and were mistreated or killed if they fell behind or showed signs of weakness.

The Bataan Death March lasted for several days. Throughout the march, the prisoners endured extreme heat, dehydration, and exhaustion. Many of them had already suffered from hunger and disease during their time in Bataan.

The Japanese guards were cruel and callous towards their captives. They would beat and kill anyone who couldn't keep up with the pace. Some prisoners were even bayoneted or shot for attempting to escape or steal food.

The prisoners faced unimaginable hardships during the march. Many of them had open wounds and infections that went untreated. They were forced to walk barefoot, and their deteriorating physical condition made each step a painful struggle. Some prisoners resorted to desperate measures like drinking their own urine or eating whatever they could find to survive.

Despite the immense suffering, the prisoners displayed extraordinary resilience and bravery. They found ways to support and encourage each other, sharing whatever food and water they had. Their camaraderie and determination provided solace during the darkest moments of the march.

When the survivors finally reached Camp O'Donnell, their ordeal was far from over. The overcrowded and unsanitary conditions at the camp led to the outbreak of diseases such as malaria and dysentery. Many prisoners, weakened by the march, died within days of arriving at the camp.

The Bataan Death March left a lasting impact on the survivors. It is estimated that around 5,000-10,000 Filipinos and approximately 500-650 Americans died during the march or in the subsequent months at Camp O'Donnell. The atrocities committed during this event were later recognized as war crimes.

In 1945, the tide of the war shifted, and General Douglas MacArthur's forces returned to the Philippines. The surviving prisoners of war were finally liberated and received medical attention and care. The Bataan Death March became a symbol of resilience and sacrifice, reminding us of the bravery and endurance of those who fought in World War II.

The Bataan Death March teaches us about the importance of remembering and honoring the sacrifices made by those who fought for freedom. The survivors of the march and their stories serve as a reminder of the resilience of the human spirit, even in the face of unimaginable adversity.

# STORY 19:

# Why Was the Battle of Stalingrad So Crucial?

In the summer of 1942, a fierce battle took place in the city of Stalingrad, located in the Soviet Union, during World War II. The battle was between the Soviet Union and Nazi Germany. Adolf Hitler, the leader of Nazi Germany, sought to take control of Stalingrad as it was an important industrial center and a symbol of Soviet resistance.

The Battle of Stalingrad was one of the deadliest battles in history, with both sides enduring heavy casualties. The battle lasted for months and was fought street by street, building by building. The Soviet forces, under the leadership of General Georgy Zhukov, defended the city with great determination, refusing to surrender.

The German forces, commanded by General Friedrich Paulus, launched a massive attack on Stalingrad. They aimed to capture the city and weaken the Soviet Union's resolve. The Germans initially had superior firepower and air support, which allowed them to make significant gains.

However, the Soviet troops fought back tenaciously. They utilized the crumbling buildings and narrow streets to their advantage, launching surprise attacks on the German forces. The Soviet soldiers also endured harsh winter conditions as the battle extended into the winter months. This familiarity with the cold weather gave them an advantage over the German soldiers.

As the battle continued, it became clear that Stalingrad would not be easily won by the Germans. Joseph Stalin, the leader of the Soviet Union, ordered that the city be defended at all costs. The Soviet soldiers displayed incredible bravery and resilience, refusing to surrender despite overwhelming odds.

In November 1942, the tide began to turn in favor of the Soviet Union. The Red Army launched a massive counteroffensive, encircling the German forces in

Stalingrad. The Germans found themselves trapped, cut off from supplies and reinforcements, surrounded on all sides.

Although outnumbered and facing starvation, the German forces persisted and held on for months. However, their situation grew increasingly desperate. The Soviet Union launched relentless attacks, gradually pushing the German troops back.

By February 1943, the German forces were on the verge of collapse. General Friedrich Paulus and his troops faced severe shortages of ammunition, food, and supplies. On February 2nd, 1943, General Paulus eventually surrendered. This surrender dealt a devastating blow to Nazi Germany and marked a crucial turning point in the war on the Eastern Front.

The Battle of Stalingrad was a significant victory for the Soviet Union. It not only halted the German advance into the Soviet Union but also lifted the morale of the Soviet people. The battle demonstrated that the German army was not invincible and that the Soviet Union could successfully resist and defeat them.

This battle served as a turning point in World War

II, weakening Nazi Germany's military power and instilling hope among the Allies for ultimate victory. It also showcased the formidable strength and determination of the Soviet Union, which played a vital role in the eventual defeat of Nazi Germany.

The Battle of Stalingrad remains an enduring symbol of courage, resilience, and sacrifice. It serves as a reminder of the indomitable human spirit's ability to endure and overcome even the harshest circumstances. The brave soldiers who fought in this battle will forever be honored, and their sacrifices will be remembered in history.

# STORY 20:

# What Role Did Women Play in the War?

During World War II, many courageous women stepped up to serve their country in the United States Army. The Women's Army Corps (WAC) was established on May 15, 1942, and it provided an opportunity for women to serve in a variety of roles and support the war effort.

Before the creation of the WAC, women had limited roles in the military, primarily serving as nurses or in administrative positions. However, with the war demanding more personnel, the need for women to contribute in other areas became evident.

The WAC recruited women from all over the country, offering them a chance to serve in diverse capacities. These women took on positions such as typists, clerks, drivers, radio operators, mechanics, and even parachute riggers. They underwent extensive training and played a vital part in ensuring the military functioned efficiently.

One of the significant contributions of the WAC was in the field of communications. With the advancement of technology during the war, the military relied heavily on radio communication. WAC members were trained as skilled radio operators, responsible for transmitting important messages between military units. Their work was crucial in coordinating operations and ensuring effective communication in the field.

The WAC also played a significant role in the medical field. Many women served as nurses, providing care for wounded soldiers on the front lines and in military hospitals. They worked tirelessly to save lives and provide comfort to those in need.

Another group of women in the WAC took on demanding roles as mechanics. They received training in repairing and maintaining vehicles and aircraft, ensuring that military equipment was ready for action. These women proved themselves just as competent as their male counterparts in this traditionally male-dominated field.

The women who joined the WAC faced numerous challenges and prejudices both at home and within the military. Some male soldiers doubted their abilities and questioned their dedication. However, through their hard work and dedication, the women of the WAC quickly earned the respect of their fellow soldiers.

In addition to their military duties, many WAC members also participated in volunteer work and community outreach programs. They provided support and assistance to military families, organized recreational activities, and even helped with public relations efforts.

The contributions of the women in the WAC were essential in helping the United States achieve victory in World War II. Their commitment and sacrifice paved the way for future generations of women to serve in the military and pursue their dreams.

Today, women serve in all branches of the U.S. military and hold positions previously reserved only for men. The Women's Army Corps played a crucial role in breaking down barriers and proving that women are just as capable as men in serving their country.

The brave women of the Women's Army Corps will always be remembered for their extraordinary efforts during World War II. Their stories inspire us to challenge stereotypes and fight for equality, reminding us that regardless of our gender, we all have the potential to make a difference.

# STORY 21:

# What Was the Last Major German Offensive?

The Battle of the Bulge was a significant event during World War II. It took place from December 16, 1944, to January 25, 1945, and was the last major German offensive on the Western Front. This battle was named "the Bulge" because of the way the front line looked on a map, where the German forces had created a bulge in the Allied lines. Let's explore the story of this intense and crucial battle.

By late 1944, the Allies had made significant progress in liberating Europe from Nazi control. However, Adolf Hitler and his generals planned one last desperate offensive to try to turn the tide of the war in their favor. The Germans believed that if they could capture the Belgian city of Antwerp, it would severely disrupt the Allies' supply lines and possibly lead to a negotiated peace.

On December 16, 1944, under the cover of heavy fog, German forces launched a surprise attack on the Ardennes Forest in Belgium. This area had been considered a relatively calm sector of the front, and the Allies were caught off guard. General Gerd von Rundstedt and Field Marshal Walter Model led the German offensive.

The German forces were formidable, including several experienced units and elements of the notorious SS divisions. They encountered relatively little resistance initially, as the Allies were caught off balance. The Germans advanced swiftly, creating a bulge in the Allied lines, which coined the term "the Battle of the Bulge."

However, the weather conditions worked against the Germans. The fog lifted, and Allied air superiority came into play. Despite initial success, the Germans were soon met with fierce resistance from the American troops, who were determined to halt their advance.

In the days and weeks that followed, the Battle of the

Bulge became a grueling and bitter fight. Communication between the Allied forces was disrupted, and many American soldiers found themselves isolated and surrounded by the German forces. There were instances of extreme bravery and heroic actions as the Allied troops fought to hold their ground and protect key strategic positions.

The Allied forces, under the command of General Dwight D. Eisenhower, swiftly organized a counterattack. American troops, including the revered 101st Airborne Division, rushed to reinforce the front lines. Despite the difficult circumstances, the Allied soldiers demonstrated incredible resilience and determination.

Through courageous efforts, the Allied forces managed to hold their positions and ultimately push back the Germans. The Battle of the Bulge was a turning point in the war, marking the beginning of the end for Nazi Germany. The offensive resulted in heavy losses for both sides, with tens of thousands of casualties.

The Battle of the Bulge was a desperate but unsuccessful attempt by the Germans to regain control of the Western Front. The resilience and bravery of the Allied troops, combined with superior air power, ultimately led to their victory. This significant battle serves as a testament to the courage and determination of the soldiers who fought during World War II.

# STORY 22:

# What Happened on D-Day?

During World War II, the Allies were determined to liberate Europe from the grip of Nazi Germany. And one of the most significant battles was the Allied invasion of Normandy, France, known as D-Day.

By 1944, the Allies had been planning this major operation for months. The goal was to establish a beachhead in France and push back the German forces. On June 6, 1944, the time had come.

Early on that fateful morning, thousands of Allied troops from the United States, Britain, and Canada boarded ships and landed on the beaches of Normandy. The sheer size and scale of the operation were staggering. It involved over 5,000 ships and boats, and nearly 156,000 troops were involved in the invasion.

The landings took place on five different beaches, each with a codename – Omaha, Utah, Gold, Juno, and Sword. The German forces heavily defended the beaches, but the Allies had carefully planned their approach. They wanted to surprise the Germans and gain a foothold on the mainland.

The assault began with intense naval bombardments designed to weaken the German defenses. However, due to poor weather and strong German resistance, the initial objectives weren't fully achieved. The troops faced heavy fire as they stormed the beaches, making it a terrifying and challenging mission. But they were determined to succeed.

On Omaha Beach, the American soldiers faced especially brutal opposition. German machine guns fired relentlessly, and many soldiers lost their lives in the chaos. Despite the overwhelming challenges, the bravery and determination of the Allied forces were unwavering.

As the days went on, the Allies gained ground and pushed deeper into France. They faced fierce resistance from the German forces, but their strength in numbers and superior firepower eventually overwhelmed the enemy. The Normandy Invasion marked a turning point in the war as the Allies gained a crucial foothold in Europe.

The success of D-Day was not achieved without losses. Thousands of brave soldiers lost their lives, and many more were injured. But their sacrifices ultimately paved the way for the liberation of Europe from Nazi control.

D-Day was a meticulously planned operation, and it required the coordination and cooperation of soldiers, sailors, and airmen from different countries. The bravery and determination of the Allied troops were instrumental in the success of the mission.

After the invasion, the Allies continued to advance through France, eventually liberating Paris and driving the Germans out of the country. It was a significant blow to Hitler and his forces and brought renewed hope to the people of Europe.

D-Day, the Normandy Invasion, exemplified the courage and determination of the Allied troops. It was a monumental event that played a vital role in the eventual defeat of Nazi Germany. The memory of those who fought on the beaches of Normandy will forever be honored for their courage and sacrifice in the fight for freedom.

# STORY 23:

# How Were the Concentration Camps Liberated?

During World War II, the Nazis established concentration camps to imprison and persecute millions of innocent people, including Jews, Romani people, political dissidents, and others considered undesirable. These camps were places of immense suffering and death. However, as the war neared its end, the Allies, fighting against the Nazis, made a remarkable and courageous effort to liberate those imprisoned in these camps.

In 1945, as the Allied forces pushed deeper into German-occupied territory, they encountered camps that revealed the horrifying extent of Nazi cruelty. They discovered places like Auschwitz, Bergen-Belsen, and Dachau, which had become synonymous with unimaginable suffering. The Allies were shocked and appalled by the conditions they witnessed – emaciated prisoners, mass graves, and evidence of systematic extermination.

Upon discovering the camps, the Allied soldiers did everything they could to help the prisoners and provide them with immediate medical care and food. Many prisoners were weak, malnourished, and suffering from diseases. The Allies worked tirelessly to bring hope and relief to those who had endured unimaginable torture and torment for years.

Medical teams were sent in to treat the sick and starving survivors. Doctors and nurses provided medical care, distributed food, and did their best to restore their physical well-being. The liberation did not only mean freedom from the Nazis but also the opportunity for survivors to regain their health and start anew.

While the prisoners were grateful for their freedom, their liberation presented a new set of challenges. Many had lost their families and homes, and they faced the daunting task of rebuilding their lives. The Allies offered support, creating makeshift displaced person camps to provide shelter, clothing, and basic necessities. They also worked to reunite families or help survivors find new homes in other countries.

The liberation of the concentration camps stands as a stark reminder of the evils of war and the atrocities committed during World War II. The Allies' efforts to rescue and care for the survivors demonstrated their commitment to justice and humanity. It is a testament to the resilience and strength of the human spirit that so many survivors were able to rebuild their lives and share their stories, ensuring that the memory of the Holocaust lives on as a lesson for future generations.

The liberation of the concentration camps was a pivotal moment in World War II. The Allies' discovery and subsequent rescue of prisoners from Nazi camps revealed the horrifying truth of the Holocaust to the world. Despite the immense challenges faced by both the survivors and the liberating forces, their commitment to justice and rebuilding continues to inspire and remind us of the importance of compassion, empathy, and the fight against prejudice and discrimination.

STUART AKOLI

# STORY 24:

# Who Were the Kamikaze Pilots?

During World War II, the Japanese military faced a significant challenge. The Allied forces had gained an advantage in the Pacific, and the Japanese were losing ground. In an effort to turn the tide of battle, the Japanese came up with a desperate and dangerous tactic - the Kamikaze pilots.

Kamikaze means "divine wind" in Japanese. The name was chosen to reflect the belief that these pilots were engaged in a special mission against the invading Allied forces and that their resolve would bring victory to Japan.

The Kamikaze pilots were primarily young men, mostly in their late teens or early twenties, who were inspired by a sense of duty and honor. They believed that sacrificing their lives for their country was the highest form of service.

To become a Kamikaze pilot, candidates had to undergo intensive training. They were taught the necessary flying skills and combat tactics, with a specific focus on carrying out suicide attacks against enemy ships. While various types of aircraft were used, including planes, helicopters, and rocket-powered gliders, the kamikaze planes were generally not stripped down of unnecessary weight, as it would have affected performance.

The first major Kamikaze attack took place in October 1944 during the Battle of Leyte Gulf in the Philippines. The Japanese launched a wave of Kamikaze pilots towards the Allied fleet, causing significant damage to numerous ships. The impact of these attacks forced the Allies to adapt their tactics and develop new strategies to counter them.

The Kamikaze pilots displayed determination and fearlessness in their missions. They would often fly at low altitudes to avoid radar detection and carefully aim their attacks with precision. Their bravery and sacrifice were acknowledged not only by their own side but also by the Allied forces, who recognized the Kamikaze pilots' unwavering dedication to their cause despite the desperate nature of their missions.

The Kamikaze attacks continued until the end of the war in 1945. While they caused substantial damage to Allied ships, they were ultimately unable to alter the outcome of the war. The United States and its Allies eventually gained the upper hand and forced Japan into surrender.

The Kamikaze pilots' willingness to sacrifice their lives for their country had a profound impact on Japanese society. Their actions were seen as heroic, and they became revered as national symbols of sacrifice. However, in retrospect, many people question the morality and effectiveness of these suicide missions.

In conclusion, the Kamikaze pilots were a unique and tragic part of World War II. Their deep dedication to their country and their unwavering commitment to give up their lives highlighted the extreme measures Japan was willing to undertake in the face of defeat. Today, the story of the Kamikaze pilots serves as a reminder of the devastating toll that war can take on those involved.

# STORY 25:

# What Made the Battle of Okinawa So Bloody?

The Battle of Okinawa was a fierce and brutal conflict that took place from April 1st to June 22nd, 1945, during World War II. It was one of the bloodiest battles in the Pacific, lasting for nearly three months and resulting in heavy casualties on both sides. Now, let's journey back in time to learn about the events that unfolded during this historic battle.

In early April 1945, Allied forces, primarily composed of American troops, launched a massive assault on the island of Okinawa. Located in the Ryukyu Islands of Japan, Okinawa was a strategic location that the Allies believed would pave the way for an eventual invasion of mainland Japan. The Japanese, aware of its importance, had heavily fortified the island and were determined to defend it at all costs.

The battle began with a relentless bombardment of Okinawa by the Allied forces. The goal was to weaken the Japanese defenses and create an opportunity for the troops to land safely. On April 1st, thousands of American soldiers stormed the beaches of Okinawa, facing fierce opposition from the well-prepared Japanese defenders.

The Japanese, under the command of Lieutenant General Mitsuru Ushijima, employed a strategy known as "shudan kodo" or "decisive battle." They planned to inflict heavy casualties on the Allies, forcing them to reconsider their invasion plans. The Japanese troops dug deep into the island's caves and tunnels, making it difficult for the enemy to dislodge them.

As the fighting intensified, both sides suffered heavy losses. The Allies faced not only Japanese soldiers but also kamikaze attacks from the sky. The Japanese had resorted to using suicide pilots who flew their planes directly into Allied ships, causing immense damage and loss of life. The bravery of these kamikaze pilots made the battle even more challenging for the Allied forces.

The struggle for control over Okinawa took a heavy toll on the civilians as well. The local population endured relentless bombing and artillery fire, leaving many without homes or basic necessities. Yet, despite the hardships they faced, the people of Okinawa showed remarkable resilience and courage.

As the battle progressed, the Allies gradually gained ground. By the end of June 1945, they had managed to secure the majority of the island, although small pockets of resistance remained. It was during these final stages of the battle that one of the most iconic photographs of World War II was taken - the image of six American soldiers raising the American flag on Mount Suribachi.

The Battle of Okinawa finally came to an end on June 22, 1945, when Lieutenant General Ushijima and his chief of staff, General Isamu Cho, were defeated by the Allies. There were no instances of ritual suicide, also known as seppuku, committed by these commanders. The battle claimed the lives of over 12,000 American soldiers, 110,000 Japanese soldiers, and a devastating number of Okinawan civilians.

The Battle of Okinawa was a significant turning point in World War II. It proved to be a critical stepping stone for the Allies towards their ultimate victory in the Pacific. The horrifying scenes and heavy casualties witnessed during this battle played a crucial role in President Harry S. Truman's decision to use atomic bombs on Hiroshima and Nagasaki, leading to Japan's surrender and the end of the war.

Today, the Battle of Okinawa is remembered as a testament to the bravery and sacrifice of those who fought on both sides. It serves as a reminder of the terrible cost of war and the importance of seeking peaceful resolutions to conflicts whenever possible.

# STORY 26:

# What Was the Impact of the Atomic Bombs?

In the final stages of World War II, when fighting between Allied forces and Japan was nearing its end, a decision was made that would forever change the course of history. The United States, seeking to bring a swift end to the war, dropped two atomic bombs on the Japanese cities of Hiroshima and Nagasaki.

On August 6, 1945, the Enola Gay, an American B-29 bomber, soared over the city of Hiroshima. At precisely 8:15 in the morning, a bomb called "Little Boy" was released and descended toward its target. The bomb exploded approximately 1,900 feet above the ground, releasing an enormous amount of energy in the form of a blinding flash of light, intense heat, and a powerful shockwave.

The destruction caused by the bomb was devastating. Buildings were reduced to rubble, and fires spread rapidly, consuming the devastated city. The bomb's impact was felt up to two miles away, with the blast wave shattering windows and causing significant damage.

In the aftermath of the bombing, an estimated 140,000 people died in Hiroshima. Many of those who survived suffered from severe burns, injuries, and radiation sickness. The effects of radiation exposure were not fully understood at the time, and even those who were farther away from the blast suffered long-term health consequences.

Just three days later, on August 9, 1945, a second bomb nicknamed "Fat Man" was dropped on the city of Nagasaki. The devastation caused by this bomb was similar to the one in Hiroshima. Approximately 70,000 people lost their lives, and thousands more were injured. The bombings of Hiroshima and Nagasaki marked the first and only use of nuclear weapons in warfare.

The decision to drop these atomic bombs was a contentious one. The intention was to force Japan to surrender, which it did on August 15, 1945, effectively ending World War II. However, the bombings raised ethical questions about the use of such a devastating weapon and highlighted the long-term consequences of nuclear warfare.

In the years that followed, the devastating impact of the atomic bombings became clear. Survivors, known as hibakusha, faced ongoing health issues and discrimination. The bombings also served as a stark reminder of the devastating power of nuclear weapons and fueled a global effort to prevent the use of such weapons in the future.

Today, Hiroshima and Nagasaki stand as symbols of peace, with memorials and museums paying tribute to the victims and emphasizing the importance of working towards a world free from the threat of nuclear weapons. The bombings of Hiroshima and Nagasaki serve as a solemn reminder of the devastating consequences of war and the urgent need to strive for peace.

# STORY 27:

# How Did Berlin Fall?

In 1945, World War II was nearing its end. The Allied forces, composed of countries such as the United States, Great Britain, and the Soviet Union, were engaged in warfare against the Axis powers, with Nazi Germany at the helm. The Soviets had been advancing steadily westward through Europe and were now preparing for their final assault on the heart of Nazi Germany, the city of Berlin.

By the spring of 1945, the German capital was in disarray. Berlin, a heavily fortified city, had endured numerous attacks throughout the war, with its walls and buildings showcasing signs of the conflict. However, the Nazis were in dire straits, running short on supplies and manpower. Despite these challenges, they remained resolute in their determination to defend the capital until the bitter end.

On April 16, 1945, the Soviet Union launched its attack on Berlin. The Soviet soldiers, outnumbering and outgunning the remaining German defenders, faced a challenging battle as they pushed through the city's defenses. The Nazis put up fierce resistance, but they were ultimately overwhelmed by the superior Soviet forces.

During the battle, a highly significant moment occurred when the Soviets raised their red flag atop the Reichstag building, which served as the German parliament. This symbolic act signaled the impending defeat of the Nazis and the triumph of the Allies.

The battle for Berlin proved to be brutal and devastating. The city suffered extensive damage as the Soviets relentlessly bombarded Nazi strongholds, reducing houses, bridges, and landmarks to rubble. Civilians caught in the crossfire endured unimaginable hardships.

Meanwhile, Adolf Hitler, the leader of the Nazis, and his closest advisors remained in his bunker beneath the city. Realizing that the end was near, Hitler took his own life on April 30, 1945. With the death of their leader, the remaining Nazi forces surrendered within days.

On May 2, 1945, the Soviet Union declared victory in Berlin. The battle had been protracted and costly, but the Soviets had successfully captured the city. The fall of Berlin served as a significant turning point in the war and marked the end of Nazi Germany's reign of terror.

The consequences of Berlin's fall were far-reaching. With the capital under Soviet control, Germany was divided into East and West, with the Soviet Union administering the eastern part. This division would later contribute to the rise of the Cold War, a period of tension between the Soviet Union and the United States.

Furthermore, the fall of Berlin brought about the conclusion of World War II in Europe. The remaining Axis powers acknowledged their defeat, and surrender promptly followed. The people of Europe celebrated V-E Day on May 8, 1945, marking the victory in Europe.

Today, the fall of Berlin serves as a poignant

reminder of the bravery and sacrifices made by the Allied forces. It represents a pivotal moment in history, embodying the triumph of democracy over tyranny. The story of the final assault on Berlin by the Soviets stands as a crucial chapter within the broader narrative of World War II.

# STORY 28:

# What Marked Victory in Europe Day?

On May 8, 1945, the world rejoiced as news spread about the surrender of Nazi Germany. This day, known as Victory in Europe Day, or V-E Day, marked the end of the war in Europe and brought hope for a brighter future.

For six long years, the world had been consumed by the chaos and destruction of World War II. Adolf Hitler and his Nazi regime had unleashed terror across Europe, causing immense suffering and devastation. But on that historic day in 1945, the German forces, overwhelmed and outnumbered, finally admitted defeat.

The announcement of Germany's surrender was

made by Allied leaders, including British Prime Minister Winston Churchill and U.S. President Harry S. Truman. People all over the world eagerly waited for the news. As soon as it was announced, there were scenes of jubilation and relief. Crowds filled the streets, waving flags, singing, and dancing. Church bells rang, and sirens blared, marking the end of the war.

In cities across Europe, celebrations erupted. Streets were filled with people embracing each other, weeping tears of joy. Soldiers and civilians alike hugged and kissed, grateful that the war was finally over. Many had lost loved ones or lived in fear for years, and now they could begin to rebuild their lives.

In London, huge crowds gathered in Trafalgar Square despite the rain that poured down. The atmosphere was electric, with everyone coming together in solidarity. Prime Minister Churchill himself addressed the nation, proclaiming, "This is your victory." He spoke of the sacrifices made by the British people and paid tribute to the Allied forces who had fought so bravely.

In Paris, the capital of France, the celebrations were no less exuberant. The Champs-Élysées was filled with people who danced in the streets, with both French and American flags proudly waving side by side. People climbed onto monuments and lampposts, cheering and singing. The French had endured the harsh occupation of their country and finally felt a sense of freedom.

However, amidst the joyous celebrations, it was important to remember the countless lives lost and the immense devastation caused by the war. While the defeat of Nazi Germany brought relief, there were still many battles being fought in the Pacific against the Japanese Empire.

In the United States, President Truman reminded the American people that victory was not yet complete. He urged everyone to remain united to achieve a final triumph over Japan. The war on the Pacific Front would continue for several more months, leading to the eventual surrender of Japan after the atomic bombings of Hiroshima and Nagasaki.

V-E Day marked a turning point in history, where the forces of tyranny and oppression were finally defeated. It was a moment when the world could feel hope and believe in a future where peace and freedom prevailed.

The celebrations on V-E Day were a testament to the resilience and determination of the human spirit. People from all walks of life came together, setting aside their differences to revel in the joyous occasion. It was a day that will forever be remembered as the end of one of the darkest chapters in human history and the beginning of a new era of hope and reconstruction.

As the world celebrated V-E Day, the focus shifted toward the future. Rebuilding shattered cities, healing wounded souls, and ensuring that the horrors of war would never be repeated became paramount. The world had learned a painful lesson, and now it was time to rebuild, reconcile, and forge a path toward lasting peace.

V-E Day stands as a symbol of the triumph of good over evil, of unity and perseverance in the face of adversity. It remains an important reminder of the power of hope and the resilience of the human spirit, inspiring generations to strive for a world where peace and compassion prevail.

# STORY 29:

# What Marked Victory over Japan Day?

On August 15, 1945, people around the world rejoiced as they heard the news that Japan had surrendered, marking the end of World War II. This day became known as Victory over Japan Day, or V-J Day. It was a time of celebration and relief as the long and brutal war finally came to an end.

The war between the Allied forces (led by countries such as the United States, the United Kingdom, and the Soviet Union) and Japan had been going on for nearly six years. It had caused widespread devastation and loss of life. Japan had refused to surrender even when faced with defeat, making the war in the Pacific a prolonged and grueling conflict.

But on August 6, 1945, everything changed. The United States dropped an atomic bomb, codenamed "Little Boy," on the Japanese city of Hiroshima. The devastation caused by the bomb was unimaginable, and it forced Japan to start considering the idea of surrender. However, the Japanese government still refused to give up completely.

Then, on August 9, 1945, the United States dropped a second atomic bomb, codenamed "Fat Man," on the city of Nagasaki. The destruction caused by these two bombs was so immense that Japan could no longer ignore the reality of their situation. Finally, on August 15, 1945, Emperor Hirohito made the announcement that Japan would surrender.

People all around the world were overjoyed with the news. In the United States, spontaneous celebrations erupted in cities and towns. The streets filled with people dancing, singing, and waving flags. The war had taken a heavy toll, and the news of victory brought relief and hope for a better future. Similar scenes of jubilation and relief played out in many other countries as well.

The official surrender ceremony took place on September 2, 1945, aboard the USS Missouri, a battleship in Tokyo Bay. General Douglas MacArthur, the Supreme Commander of the Allied forces in the Pacific, presided over the ceremony. On behalf of the Allied nations, he accepted Japan's formal surrender. This momentous event marked the end of World War II.

However, the war's impact remained deeply felt. Millions of lives had been lost, and many cities lay in ruins. It would take years for nations to rebuild and heal from the devastation. The war had profoundly changed the world, and its effects would be felt for generations to come.

Today, V-J Day serves as a reminder of the sacrifices made by those who fought and the lasting peace that came after such a devastating war. It is a day to honor the courage and resilience of the individuals who served during World War II, as well as the countless civilians who endured hardships and supported the war effort.

As we remember Victory over Japan Day, let us not forget the lessons learned from this chapter in history. May we strive to build a world where peace and understanding prevail, and may we cherish the freedom we enjoy today because of the sacrifices made by those who came before us.

# STORY 30:

# What Were the Nuremberg Trials About?

During World War II, Adolf Hitler and the Nazi party committed terrible crimes against humanity. They started a war, invaded countries, and carried out the systematic genocide of millions of innocent people, particularly targeting Jewish people. When the war finally ended in 1945, the world was left to deal with the aftermath of these atrocities.

In November 1945, the Nuremberg Trials were held in the city of Nuremberg, Germany. These trials aimed to bring to justice those responsible for the crimes committed during the war. The trials were significant because they set a precedent for holding individuals accountable for their actions during times of war.

The Nuremberg Trials were conducted by an international military tribunal made up of judges from the United States, the Soviet Union, Great Britain, and France. The prosecutors presented evidence against 24 high-ranking Nazi officials, including Hermann Göring, who was a prominent member of the Nazi regime.

The trials focused on three main charges: crimes against peace, war crimes, and crimes against humanity. Crimes against peace referred to the planning, preparation, initiation, and waging of wars of aggression. War crimes included atrocities committed against prisoners of war, civilians, and others. Crimes against humanity encompassed acts committed against any civilian population, including murder, extermination, enslavement, and persecution.

The prosecutors had the enormous task of presenting evidence to prove the guilt of the accused. They presented documents, photographs, and testimonies from survivors and witnesses who had experienced the horrors of the Nazi regime firsthand. The defendants were given a fair trial with the opportunity to defend themselves, but many of them were unable to deny their involvement in the crimes.

The Nuremberg Trials were not just about punishing the perpetrators of war crimes. They were also an opportunity to establish international laws aimed at preventing future atrocities. The trials gave birth to the concept of individual criminal responsibility, stating that individuals are responsible for their own actions, regardless of orders from their superiors.

Several key moments occurred during the trials. One of the most memorable was when Göring took the stand and passionately defended his actions, claiming he had acted in the best interest of the German people. However, the evidence against him was overwhelming, and he was found guilty.

In the end, 12 of the accused were sentenced to death, 7 were given prison sentences, and 3 were acquitted. The punishments were meant to send a strong message that those who commit heinous crimes will be held accountable.

The Nuremberg Trials were an important chapter in history, as they laid the groundwork for future international courts, such as the International Criminal Court, which still exists today. They showed the world that justice could be served, even in the face of unimaginable atrocities.

While the Nuremberg Trials cannot undo the suffering and loss caused by the Nazi regime, they provided a sense of closure for the victims and their families. They also emphasized the importance of learning from the past and ensuring that such crimes are never repeated.

The legacy of the Nuremberg Trials lives on, serving as a reminder of the horrors of war and the necessity of holding individuals accountable for their actions. It is a testament to the resilience of humanity and our ongoing commitment to justice and peace.

# CONCLUSION

As we reach the end of our journey through the most defining moments of World War II, it's clear that this period in history is marked by unparalleled bravery, sacrifice, and resilience. The stories of those who lived through these events—soldiers on the front lines, civilians enduring the horrors of war, and leaders making pivotal decisions—serve as powerful reminders of the strength of the human spirit.

Reflecting on the intense battles, strategic operations, and personal narratives, we gain a deeper appreciation for the complexities and hardships of war. These stories not only highlight the profound impacts on the individuals involved but also demonstrate how their actions collectively shaped the world we live in today. From the beaches of Normandy to the streets of Berlin, the courage and determination displayed continue to inspire and teach valuable lessons about perseverance, unity, and hope.

The experiences of World War II are a testament to the enduring will to overcome adversity. As we remember these moments and the people who lived them, we honor their legacy and ensure that their sacrifices are never forgotten. The history of World War II is not just a collection of dates and events but a tapestry of human experiences that continue to resonate through the generations.

In exploring these tales of heroism and hardship, may we be inspired to carry forward the principles of peace, justice, and resilience. Let these stories serve as a beacon, guiding us toward a future where the lessons of the past strengthen our resolve to build a better world for all.